Kindling

by Mary Dorcey

Published by Onlywomen Press Ltd.,
38 Mount Pleasant, London WC1.

ISBN 0 906500 09 5

Copyright © Mary Dorcey 1982

All rights reserved. No part of this book may be reproduced in any form without written permission of Onlywomen Press Ltd.

Cover design by Robyn Sivewright

Typesetting by Dark Moon
Cover printed by Chromocraft Ltd.
Printed by Onlywomen Press Ltd.

Mary Dorcey was born in Ireland in 1950, and grew up in County Dublin where she attended convent school. She has lived in France, England, Japan and the U.S.A. A founder member of Irish Women United, Mary has been active in the Women's Liberation Movement since 1972. Her work has been published in feminist journals in Ireland, England and America and she has given readings in all these countries. She's currently living in London.

Some of the poems in KINDLING first appeared in the following publications; *Vision of Revolution* in Irishwomen's Diary 1982 and in WICCA, *In a Dublin Nursing Home* in Spare Rib, *Coming Home* and *After Long Absence* in Spinster (UK) and Plexus (USA), *Blood Relations* in Spinster, *Night Protest* in Off Our Backs (USA), *Friendship* in WICCA.

Contents

After Long Silence	7
Coming Home	8
Blood Relations	11
Woman in a Normandy Field	12
In a Dublin Nursing Home	13
Evening	15
Full Circle	16
Vision of Revolution	18
Colonised Minds	20
America	21
The Quarrel	22
Mirrors	25
Rope	26
Spring	34
Night	35
Party	36
Photographs	37
Autumn	39
Words without Echo	40
Before the Tide	41
April Afternoon	43
Night Protest	44
Friendship	46
House in Winter	47

After Long Silence

We regard each other
awkwardly, speechless
we who have so much
to unsay
to forget or at least forgive.

And then
in unconscious diplomacy,
with that old grace
that so often came
between you and your consequences

You stretch your hand
to mine
and some ember of the me
that I was to you,
rekindles
and in silence,
recovers the power of
speech.

Coming Home

Coming home
the streets seem more narrow than ever.
The crowds terrifying in their intimacy,
at any moment a face may attack
demanding familiarity, ensnaring me
in our collective past.
Having trusted for so long
to the implacable indifference
of New York city strangers, to cross
now the paths of Stephen's Green,
feels like walking naked
through a relative's cocktail party.

Waiting the prescribed half hour for my
bus, i note signs of capitalist progress;
the large stores devouring the smaller,
rows of Georgian houses gaping
like a mouth of rotting teeth.
Shop fronts display a new risqué image,
the black tie and waistcoat that
so shocked my lover's family last year
now flaunted by Switzers' most elegant
dummies, a discreet lesbian touch
at last fit for bourgeois seduction.
And everywhere the resentful eyes of

Men, unable to lift their gaze
from women who dare to ignore them.
The busman's insistent *'Love'* and *'Dear'*
turns to a snarl of *'Fucking whore'*
when i tell him at thirty i'm not a girl.
The publican lusts for an excuse to
refuse me a pint, while the lads rest
their bellies against the bar, a
civilian militia to enforce female servility.
At the back of their bitter eyes, the old
fear flickers a little nearer the surface.
A young nun passes by me, and gives

A half hearted conciliatory smile,
no longer quite certain that this mortal
evidence of God's love can appease
the rancour of a disappointed world.
So i make my way to a bookshop
which provides in this town
one respected refuge
from the idle malice of its curiosity.
And i find a small women's section,
poetry, novels, political papers,
giving proof of the sustained struggle
of some irish women against

The vicious bigotry of all the pope's boys
on this island, their Maginot line.
And of course i meet an old friend
who invites me for a drink and gives
me all the gossip just short of scandal,
reminding me how charmed is the protective
circle we've built in this small place
that unwillingly, yet so successfully
still breeds creative eccentricity.
As the light falls to the vivid auburn
of a Dublin city evening
and secretaries at last set loose

March towards their flats intent on tea,
i turn my collar against the wind
curse my bare head and my forgetfulness
that whatever the morning sky, that
depression moving from the west always
carries rain. And suddenly i hear a cry
a rebel word across the air, and turning see
a woman selling papers, lifted high, in the
street's damp darkness brandished like a torch.
We smile at one another in salute
while our ancient name *'Wicca'*, *'Wicca'*,
challenges the night.

Blood Relations

Leaving
she bends to kiss you
slowly on each cheek,
drawing closer to let slip
a few last words
in your foreign tongue
and i, discreet,
embarrassed to be the chosen
the one who stays,
lower my eyes and pretend indifference
granting her one last intimacy.

Can you blame me then
if i forget,
that it is only your mother
saying goodbye after morning coffee
whose eyes as they acknowledge mine
are brilliant with shamed jealousy.

Woman in a Normandy Field

She stood alone
under a grey sky's impassive discipline,
dark earth stretched about her beyond sight
    its raw furrows gaping.
Turning full circle she surveyed a year's work
    laid out like a cloth before her.
Then slowly her knees bent to ground once more
    and with deliberate hands
she began the season's first task.

In a Dublin Nursing Home

Our hands clasped together on the white sheet
seemed to tick soft and loud as a time bomb
in the sterilized cosiness of that place.
'No sickness or grief here please', where
wounds are freshly dressed each day and
nights are tucked in with 'little sleepers',
in wards made crisp with daffodils,
aflutter with nurses who smooth every doubt
with solicitous smiles impeccably starched.

The golf course stretches green and calm
outside the picture windows, a gentle
reminder of the virtues of health so
cheerfully guarded in the real world, while
tired voices conscious of ingratitude, agree
with sister that yes the lawns are splendidly kept.
Husbands come and go, devotion comfortably
contained within the appropriate visiting hours,
and the roses stacked above yesterday's roses

Stare from their lockers blank as photos in a
family album. As evening comes the television
chatter shrouds our fitful conversation,
but our hands embracing on the white sheet
vibrate with a violence that we know must pierce
each tactful barricade of earphone and raised
newspaper. And when at last i leave, i am stalked by
every eye, until Mrs. Kavanagh the chosen mediator,

Exorcizing any shadow of disquiet
in a voice made suave with homeliness
declares — *'You have a lovely sister!'*
But that last night,
strained beyond embarrassment or caution
when i took your face between my hands
and kissed your mouth a slow good bye,
it seemed the bomb would explode
in a shower of brilliant sparks that

Might have set the ward alight were
it not for the immediate action of fire-
fighting nurses, who with the ice composure
of a lifetime's training in temperature control
drew screens, plumped pillows, inserted
thermometers, and asked me to wait outside
while they changed your dressings.
But one young nurse arriving too hurriedly, with
her face and her uniform not yet fully buttoned

Carelessly looked in our eyes as we parted
and for once confronted too soon for defence
stood aghast as routine collapsed.
Her jaws shuddered and starch began to run
from her lips in thick white tears
her limp face gazed about unchecked and
in that moment, stripped of her smile
she saw sickness, grief and passion
— undressed.

Evening

Outside my window
the curve of the hills
intimate as a lover's body,
violet clouds sail
almost brushing the hedges
like soap bubbles blown by a child.

Your fingers trace old histories
drawing memory from my skin
as easily as they would a thorn.

Sparrows gossip
on a spider black branch
taunting a thin cat,
and as the day's last shadow
lights your face
i kiss your breast again
and solemnly promise
to get up early tomorrow.

Full Circle

We have closed the circle.
The wheel that spun us dizzy for five
years through all the set phases
of love and rejection.
Having survived a near fatal attraction
have I lived to be crippled by what seems
incurable liking?
It was obvious from the first or so they say.
We met, touched and lurched into love, when
the fever dropped we faced each other
cold headed strangers.
Some mischievous impulse drove us to

Retrace our steps and we found ourselves
at our starting point — charmed and curious.
It was easy then to be caught in the
final snare — the kind of passionate
sympathy for which one still imagines
a lifetime too short.
And it did after all get us through
four seasons, before jealousy struck
blasting us into little fragments,
each bone chip with a separate grievance.
We might have settled then for the peace of
hatred but fatalism or some higher vision

Lured us back into wary alliance, until
we acknowledged or resigned ourselves
to a friendship that seemed proved beyond
all vagaries of politics and lust.
Then was it because no outside force
remained to threaten us,
that you with your craving for destruction,
incubated an infection that spread like
cancer through all our words of love
and comfort until our breath stank.
And there was nothing left for us
but to cut through skin and tissue

Until we reached the heart.
Six months later, sleeping
once more because I have no longer
anything left to dream of you,
I woke this morning and thought I felt
your hand, soft and confiding as on the first
and last day it held mine.
But no matter — I never did heal quickly.
My nerves still bear the scar of a tooth
pulled in childhood and each winter
it stabs me awake
on the first cold October morning.

Vision of Revolution

Grey flakes of snow straggle
Into pools on the streets of Dublin, on this
The first of May — International Labour Day.
    Wind like a scythe cuts over the Liffey
    Shaving the reddened ears of marching workers
Who led by the drums of a union band, strut
Beneath their banners four abreast with
Shoulders raised, fists pumping at their sides.
Armed in black and grey their eyes keep step,
Resisting all trivial distraction as
    They march towards their promised new order
    With grim mechanical discipline,
Having no vision of power or pride
Free of uniforms and military hymns. Then

As they cross O'Connell bridge i see their
Ranks are broken by bursts of bright colour
— Red coats and blue umbrellas — as arm in arm
    The women come, like daisies that break to air
    Between concrete pavement slabs.
Waving their placards to passers-by
Loitering to chat with friends in the crowd
On holiday from work for one afternoon,
Mischievous as sparrows in this virile solemnity.
'Move along girls please — this isn't a picnic'
    A union steward reinforces order —
    Eyes blunt with resentment,
Remembering no doubt the dignity of his past
When men made politics and women made tea.

Well boys — it seems
You've got some explaining to do,
You'd better make it clear
   To them right from the start
   That revolutions were never made for fun.
There be no laughter at the barricades.
And while you prepare for your justice day —
The birth of the workers' dictatorship,
There can be no erosion of your strength
Till then *'slaves of slaves'* they must remain.
   And as for this talk of consciousness-raising,
   Can there really be the least doubt
That anything but bourgeois decadence is encouraged
When slaves begin to sing in their chains?

Colonised Minds

Men are the enemy.
Isn't that what we used to say?
And wasn't it all so easy

Back in those innocent days?
Well the years have changed us
Of course, and we all compromise

If we're able, and i measure
The state of our cynicism these days
By the remarks we let pass at table.

Such as at that dinner for Mother's
Day, we gave for your lover
And her child, when you toasted her

With your wine and a smile, saying
'Here's to all mothers'
And she with that cheap innuendo

That here passes for sexual guile,
Leered into your eyes for reply
And said *'Here's to the mother fucker!'*

So are we only to find, having set
Men aside, that safe in our lesbian
World we speak with their voices,

And *'fuck'* with their minds?
Oh wasn't it all so easy
Back in those innocent days,

When we thought only men
Were the enemy and not
— The women they've made.

America

They had boasted it
as something special, an ancient house
in the European style.
As I entered the old rooms and felt
their years cluster about me
I was at peace for the first time.
I gazed out the dark windows, sheltered
by the knowledge that I was just one
of so many others, to have watched these
great trees do battle with the wind

Or heard their leaves break and fall
in an autumn dusk.
And I understood then the loneliness
that I feel in this brash new country,
where everything is being done
as though never before.
Where there are no other presences
to keep me company,
no guiding hand in shadow at an open
door. No echo beneath our talk

Of those other inhabitants
— the half-seen face in the glass
— the sigh of their lost conversation,
reminding me that we are not alone
and need not struggle so anxiously
always to be first or last.
I miss those presences, quiet about me.
Here in this young country it seems
the air is too thin to fill lungs
grown rich with the breath of ghosts.

The Quarrel

It had started so well — a warm night,
the winding streets bright with voices
the smell of coffee in the air.
'A good movie maybe' (we should know by now)
'And afterwards dinner in some left bank restaurant.'
— A quiet table, good wine, greek salad
everything right,
and then was it because I ate too fast
or because you pretended to catch my joke,
or had one more misogynist film

Soured us more than we knew?
Some unguided word — complaint, rebuke,
a plate pushed aside, voices too loud
and suddenly all Paris was a gaping,
mocking eye, other people — straight
people — shocked from their dinners.
We might have hidden your tears
but my stiff averted face, what kind
of woman ignores another's tears?
You stumbled into the street — I followed,

Some stupid man — his pity pouncing
— *'Go to hell'*
'Please don't get into a fight'
'Don't try to control me, I'll do what I like'
'So have it your way, I'll go then'
'Yes go — go now!'
And I meant what I said, better,
much better alone — unfettered, what did I care, with all
Paris brilliant before me, the air rich

Faces strung like lights along the river,
it's sinuous path binding the crowds together.
I leant over the bridge and watched
the *bateau mouche* go by, with its cargo
of respectably festive people, people who
can be counted on to enjoy what they pay for.
And suddenly the smooth stone was cold
under my hand, and turning to look after
you, found you — nowhere — out of sight.
My eyes ran to the metro and back,

The whole street was empty of you.
The stone cold against my touch,
the bright lights paling on the dark water.
A small child stared up at me
hurried on by his father — something unseemly
then in my face. Unfit for children.
I looked about slowly, forcing myself
to concentrate — appreciate — the great buildings,
their tall implacable facades
their pallid skin. The bridges arching

Over the river — lover over lover.
Lights everywhere, noise, cafes, laughter,
the whole city thick with stale beauty,
it's grandeur and decadence alike
condemning me — alone.
'Ca va Mademoiselle,' — another smiling
carnivore in at the kill.
Don't get into a fight you said
so alright I'll be good, hide my eyes,
their sorrow raw meat in a zoo.

Pushing my way through, shrunk to an invisible
core, women chattering, men leering
Cheer up, have a coffee — a beer? My last
night after all in this city of romance.
At the metro suddenly — my shoulders are
cold. Admit defeat, why not go home?
Down the stairs a woman plays the flute
its notes like water through the dry tunnels.
She smiles and I too
but the coins I drop are guilt that tonight

I've shut myself out from such innocence.
Finally on your street, having no key I
telephone (your house, your city — every advantage)
your voice at last, uncertain, no worse.
I walk slowly, postponing further recrimination
or a too easy release?
Fucked up again, my fault I know,
What price apologies as cafes begin to close?
Then at the courtyard door you stand
head to one side — the smile at your mouth

Will it reach your eyes? Our bodies draw close
— a moment's stiffness, then your arms
are about me, your warmth — your strength
and our mouths open to one another.
You hold me and rock me, laughing 'Come
for a drink', not too late yet in this city
of romance. And standing unable to part
our blood beating out hurt and anger, I know
that it is still good — in the magic of childhood
our wounds heal at touch.

Mirrors

At the foot of your garden
The sea plunges in its narrow bed.
Stilled by its clamour you stand,

Peonies and lupin that he planted
The year of his death, each summer
Recover their place about you. You

Have grown old in their light. You
Have watched your children go from
You and said no word to halt them. You

Have friends and books — money enough
A good neighbour to one side — six
Grandchildren. But your daughters will

Never marry now and you will never
See your eyes shine from the faces of
Their daughters. This one regret

You hold in silence, for you have other
Windows to the world, through which you
Glimpse a life and loves not spoken of

In well curtained drawingrooms. I
Walk from you with my woman lover
Down the smooth flower lined path,

Your smile follows me to the gate and
No stranger passing could tell what
Dark pleasures are mirrored in your eyes.

Rope
For Cheryl R. 1979

It is dark and quiet here
In these white lit corridors.
Our feet shuffle their despair
Across smooth nylon lawns,
We glide our misery through polished doors
That swing noiseless at our touch.
The gleaming walls are fat and soft
Around our hopelessness.
We do not hear each other scream
Those of us who still scream . . .

It is dark and peaceful here
In these cool, heat filled passage ways
That stretch long and flat without
A twist or shadow.
We walk to and fro, fro and to
In ones and twos and threes —
We giggle and cry and belch.
We rock each other's pain, out and in
With silent hands
We dribble now and then and wail.

Our eyes have long since lost the nervous
Habit of outside eyes —
The awkward twitch and hover —
The struggle to remain, outside.
We gaze wide and slow, pupils quiet as stones.
Blood holds no terror for us
And tears we drink in plastic cups
Sweet as the milky tea, we buy
Our visitors in the recreation lounge.
It is calm and shallow here

The dark green plants hang limp
The chapel door is ajar — a jar.
My jaws are stiff these days
I slur and slop my words,
It startles her and him when they
Come to view.
Tranquil tranquil pills for peace
Pink pills for lock jaw, blue for sleep
Green for saliva running down your
Chin. Red for screams and coma.

It is dark and noiseless here
I will not stir today.
My bed is warm and dry, my slippers
Wait by the door.
I have lucozade and magazines
And coloured sweets piled high, in my
Steel without stain ashtray.
The pills I save each morning, I count out
On the sheet — white and pink and blue
As the smiling cheeks about me.

Perhaps he will come today
It is a Sun day there.
I will wash my face at a quarter to three
My dress is pressed and still, in my bedside closet.
Evelyn screamed all night, last night
It broke my sleep — my eyes are ringed
Today she's laughing loud, going home
For her children's party.
Moods sail like clouds here, hazy and light
It is such a long time since I screamed;

My face a gorged jelly, ripped
And wobbling, my voice like a siren
Shrilling off my head.
It was that, that finished her off — off
She will not come again.
No more needles then
Her slow thin needle piercing my brain;
'But don't you think you'd feel better
If you could only begin to try . . .'
And the short quick jab —

'Come on now really — enough is enough.'
Yes, she tried alright. They all tried.
But she tried longest.
Drilling me with her kindness and will
To change to change to change.
So many needles, short and long, quick and slow
Scraping, puncturing, bruising;
'Will want could should real wrong
Must surely right can be why not
Believe me much better if no worse,

Strength hope identity patience
Time time time time time.'
Yes they tried alright, right so right
But I kept their last needle,
Though nobody knows.
I have it safe under my pillow
The very last needle of all — time.
And I have all the time
In this world of time. Such a small
Word to hold it all,

You'd think its skin would burst
But i take good care.
How big it grows here, under my pillow
I feed it well. Each day it swells
A little fatter in the dark
With it safe I grow quiet again
Black and calm with quiet
Out there it was so sharp and white.
Perhaps if he comes
Nurse Howard will call, give me
Her smile and take me down on her arm.

My head is heavy today — it rolls a little
Like a beach ball on a deck
Ship heaving dipping swaddled by waves.
I will not stir today.
My slippers wait by the door.
So quiet, now that I have decided, not to
Decide, to decide, not to decide
To decide, not to decide
De cide no cide two sides to every question,
Or so they say.

I will count my pills again
So nice to steal their soothing colours,
I remember the days before them
When I tore and retched and spat
Blood and spittle on my shirt and skirt
The hollow gape inside me
A white mouth eating my brain and heart
Now it is still and quiet
I am the hollow — a great dark hollow
It cannot eat me now.

My eyes are black pits flat and calm
My skin shines tears leave no trace
— Their faces grow huge and pink with tears
No where to hide.
Today it is Sun day. They have come to view today
The outsiders.
Their eyes slither and crawl.
Their voices dart like birds trapped
Beating their wings on the window pane.
I like to make them dart and flutter

And watch them bashing their heads
Against my pain.
The feathers fly in my mouth
I am silent and deep. My eyes tell them nothing
I keep some feathers each week
They feed the darkness under my pillow
Time grows fat on their blood stained feathers.
Perhaps he will come today
If not I will dress for tea
And sit with Peter and Marjorie

Perhaps his green car will come. Go and come.
There was a reason once i know,
They say there is always a reason.
I waited for it for years
Each night in the dark of whiskey
And the television light.
He did not come then either
But there was a reason for waiting,
I know there was.
I drank myself to sleep each year

We went out to visit friends and relations
He talked I talked, we smiled, they smiled
No tears then for them
We ate and slept and worked and things
We went on. On.
I hung on. I was strong and brave
I gripped him like a rope — a rope
Hanging from a cliff. His cliff.
I hung on until my fingers bled and
I grew hoarse with the fight for silence

I gripped and swung blind between cliffs
I did not hear the rope tear.
I know, I did not hear it shred
They say there must always be warning
I heard nothing but the cracking noise
In my head.
And I fell — fell
Though I did not let go — I did not let go
Fell
Though I did not let go.

Somebody else cut my rope.
His eyes quiet his face white his hands clean
He tied — he held — he cut the rope
The rope of time of promise of vows
For richer for poorer in sickness in health
In sickness. For ever and ever.
Tied   held   dropped.
Nobody heard me fall. My teeth were locked.
But a white shriek cut me in two as I fell.
It must have been the rope singing

Against the rock
That brought them. The ambulance
The white coats the lights the voices
The needles. The needles long and thin
The silence the voices the darkness
The long corridors.
I never did reach the ground,
Though they say you always do
I kept on falling into space
The air spinning from me,

The cliff face racing back
Until there was only space,
Nothing but blue white air.
It is Sun day today
He might come in his grey suit
His hair and his voice brushed smooth.
Behind them I can see his face
Grown white and wrinkled now,
Crumpled with memory.
His eyes and fingers twitch from me

He smells of pain — a thin green gas.
I will not tell him that I kept the rope
The bloodstained shreds and threads
I will not tell him that.
I have stored it under my pillow
I feed it in tiny fragments to the darkness
Under my pillow.
To the dark and time.
Time grows big and fat on it
Big with feathers and the threads of our rope.

I will not tell him that or this
I am making a new one.
My rope,
Of pink and white feathers and blood
Skin   saliva   tears and silence
Screams and twitching eyes and mouths
And the shreds of our rope.
Plaiting my time — in out out in
Time empty and still
Shapeless cool and see through

How well it weaves. Clean and hollow
Without scent or colour.
No one will find this one.
No one will tie or dangle or cut — this one
I am weaving my time (just as they told me to
With their needles and pills)
A long pure line stretched wide
In these dark and silent passage ways.
I will not stir today
My slippers wait by the door.

I will tell Doctor Kelsey I rested well
That will please. I will rest and wait.
Till he comes. If not
I will wash my face   black and clean for supper
I will sit with John and Rosemary
And wait for tomorrow
Perhaps there'll be ice cream for dessert
I scream   white and pink
I will swallow it down to my darkness
Cool and smooth and white.

Spring

The coming of spring
has quickened my ears,
and i hear faint sounds
that the snow of winter
muffled,
the cry of sea birds
on the coast,
and the harshness that now
edges your voice.

Night

I remember your neck, its strength
and the sweetness of the skin at your throat.
I remember your hair, long, in our way
drawing it back from my mouth.
How my hands slid the low plain of your back
thrown by the sudden flaunt of your loins.
I remember your voice,
the first low break
and at last the long flight
loosing us to darkness.
And your lips along my shoulder,
more sure, even than i had imagined,
how i guarded their track.

I ask you then
what am i to do with all these memories
heavy and full?
Hold them, quiet, between my two hands,
as i would if i could again
your hard breasts?

Party

Through the noise and laughter
loneliness creeps in, like
a cold breeze on a summer evening.

Walking into rooms and out again,
you drink to entertain your hands,
shuffle phrases, watch other people

Dance. In the smoke lit air, mouths
eat, kiss, chatter. Eyes dart like
flies, devouring each resting place.

Music stops and starts, bodies parade
their practised fever, mirror dazzled
they shine for you — you or

Anyone. Spinning high on this ferris
wheel of free choice and free love,
who dares to look down?

As we rush blind from
the chill core of the heart
we call our independence.

Photographs

On a bare boned pram a young seagull stood,
grey water slipped between rocks and tin cans
dribbling a green froth along its flanks, while
   mud coloured ducks swam among the debris
   salvaging bread from plastic wrappers.
Then i saw it — drifting on the slow current, a
woman's arm naked in the thin sunlight, and
at the water's edge, a black stockinged thigh
   half buried in mud and silt.
I looked about and saw

That rocks and sand were littered
with broken bits of flesh,
breasts and hips in white lace underwear,
   smooth brown torsos strewn idly
   among empty bottles and paper bags.
One face stared up
with a hideous lipsticked grin,
ripped from its shoulders
   yet still determined to please.
Some boys behind me shouted —

'Hey lads look at the dirty photos!' For of
course, to any normal eye they were just that
photographs — only pictures.
   Blow-ups from some glossy porno magazine
   discarded in shame or boredom
to float dismembered on the river
exposed to every vacant glance.
Whooping and sniggering
   the boys raced towards the shore but
with a shout of rage that shocked my ears

I chased them back, and struggled down
the bank's wet sand, where looking at
the first stained face, some helpless,
　　protective urge, made me kneel to gather up
　　the sodden bits and pieces of women, who they say,
had long since lost the right to care
who looked or touched. Regaining the road
I bound them tight in old newspaper
　　struck a match and watched them flame
blue green into the sunlight.

Autumn

I wish I had never seen
that smile you sent
over your lover's shoulder
to another woman's eyes,
did you have to remind me tonight
how soon the leaves fall
in this part of the country?

Words without Echo

Come then
forget that you saw it
forget that i said it,
forget the cold truths
that have come between us like glass.

Forgive the body
that has such different things to say
and only one way to say them.
Forget the old luxuries:
words without echo
eyes with no reflection.

Come then
— many flowers blossom on one stem
kiss me,
and i will not ask
why you close your eyes.

Before the Tide

A slow sea,
a long clear stretch of sand.
The usual things — glazed wood and stone,
seaweed stacked in a glistening breakwater.
Far down, near the harbour
a white dog barking at a wave.

Then — full in the sun
as if laid out to dry,
the wings of some great sea
bird — something like a cormorant
spread wide on a granite rock.
Drawing near
i see the head is twisted back
— startled by a sudden noise?

Its beak plunged between smooth
feathers — black with a sheen of purple.
At the belly a grey foot dangles
like a twig snapped in its fall.
One eye is sealed with mud,
the other staring upwards
as if the sky had frozen in it.

Overhead a hundred gulls scream
above a movement in the air,
gliding and buffeting
— not one falling.
In the fields behind
skin twitching from flies
a horse and foal stand, yellow flowers
blown about their hooves.

A low gust snatches
a tail feather and throws it
across the stones to sea.
The bird lies still.

And i stare down
at this unmoving thing
that will not flinch from wind
or human eye.
Fixed and soundless, before the tide
the only creature of its kind
as if it were
an unusual thing
to die.

April Afternoon

The tar of the roof
black and slippery wet
and the rain water dripping
from walls and gutter.
Drip, drip, dripping

From the grey slate tiles
and red brick chinmeys,
from drain pipes and
the steel ribs of t.v. aerials.
The knotted black hair

Of the winter trees,
the bald briar bushes
littered with paper bags,
all dripping.
Everything, even the wings

Of the brown sparrow
dripping on the wet telegraph
wire. Water ceaselessly
falling
in small slow drops,

Dripping from a low sky
covering the ground like mist
washing and wearing everything,
each thing in this place
into sodden acquiescence.

Night Protest

We stood outside that prison wall,
The slow rain speared by barbed wire,
Stood outside and called your name.
Called against the dark and our own dread
In the shadow of that grey stone mass,
Where each square foot of twilight
Is held behind bars.
Then through the clouded air something

Fluttered white — a strip of sheet
Or handkerchief
Making its own small peace there
By reaching out to us.
And was it your voice that broke clear?
Two hundred stood in silence but
It did not come again.
Later a cell light flashed

Once — twice — a signal surely
Or just some careless warder?
So we sang for you the old battle songs
For you who had so often stood
On both sides of this wall,
And someone set a placard burning
Sparking a passage for our voices,
And i wanted to call *'She's still*

Carrying a torch for you Marie.'
Nell cried the last message *'We'll be*
Seeing you soon again but we have
To go home for our dinners now.'
And i thought of yours that day,
Each day — the oiled tea, damp bread,
The egg and sausage floating
On a tin plate.

And i tried not to think of those other
Abuses — the little things that cripple:
The drooling eye at the peep-hole
And two sanitary towels — per woman
— Per month.
And how many others inside that fortress
Strained to hear their own name spoken?
How many others forgotten

Unknown
In for a pound of butter
Or for servicing some man in a car.
So we sang for them too
*'Oh sisters don't you weep, don't you
Moan'* and maybe they knew.
We left one by one, some still calling
A name or a joke

Moving slowly for your sake
But wanting to run from the damp
Infectious air of that place.
And the 'Branch' men sullen in their
Cars, watched us pass stiff eyed
The sense beginning to grip at last,
That they'd more than one
Brazen bitch — banging the bars.

Friendship

Although we had talked all night,
about rejection, hurt
and the bitterness of those
we had once most trusted,
lying in your arms, in a warm bed,
rummaging through our injuries
like two old drunken women on a bench,

It no longer mattered at all
— none of it.
Breast against breast
desiring nothing more than sleep,
loss was a once sharp blade
that had cut me loose
for this friendship.

House in Winter

In a cold room
dawn light stirs on skin.
Wind sucks at the roof beams,
lips to bone we rekindle
the old track of heat along the nerves.
From hand to widening eye
the spark climbs
the taut rope of your spine.
Ribs crack like tinder.

Below us
someone moves about the empty house.
Our cupped hands hold the flame
our mouths suckle it.
Footsteps mount the stairs
shudder through our breathing.
Higher and higher — they come
stumble past the door
and quicken —

My hands fly loose
your eyes catch fire.
From heart and lungs and belly
breath sings —
the air shatters
in spears of ringing crystal
blue and gold and silver.

Somewhere below
a door slams shut
returning us.
Silence seeps like snow
about the roof and walls.
But listen —

at the window
we have startled a yellow wasp
from winter.
With a fevered hum
it climbs the chill glass
beating its way to summer.

In a cold room
we reach slowly
and draw the fallen covers
up from our feet.